Ida Bohatta

Saint Nicholas
English Version by John Theobald

ars edition

Santa was once Saint Nicholas.
He has a difficult task,
But all year dreams of how it was
When wrapping the gifts that were asked.
Now he's dreaming of apples and pie
(Angels, don't wake him up)
And while he nods, a year goes by.
(Yawn!) what a lovely sleep!

The little angel breaks his heart
Because a child got such a spank.
"Why would they switch a child like that
When after all, it was only a prank?"

The saint replies, "Don't cry, don't cry!
Christmas Day will soon be here
With hardly a spank for girl or boy
And never a switch to fetch a tear!"

Saint Nicholas used to look like a king.
Wouldn't you like to help him bring
Flowers and fruit and everything?
Out in the woods the snow is deep.
Angels help too while we are asleep.

Who has tidied up a mess?
Who when asked to help said "Yes"?
Who has shared some fun with brothers?
Who has thought to pray for others?
Then you have a happy home
Where the saint will love to come.

Saint Nicholas is the secret friend
Who visits every home.
Small angels flock to help him, and
You don't know when they come.
One holds the sack wide open for
Goodies. Hey, everyone,
Look! down the road here comes some more
When these will all be gone!

From door to door Saint Nicholas goes
When all the world is still.
Here are five angels and some shoes,
Laid out for them to fill;
And there's a basket, just in case
The shoes don't hold enough.
The angels like this little place
Where children love to laugh.

This little girl is poor.
She has no presents yet.
She sits by the chapel door.
Saint Nicholas doesn't forget.
He gives her the reddest apple,
And two sweet angels come
With a sack of gifts to the chapel
And say, "Here, take every one."

"Will I be big enough next year
To help Saint Nicholas?
Can I too help him feed the poor
And little birds in the grass?"

"Yes, you don't have to be an angel;
Just listen to them sing.
They'll take you along if you join their song
Of Christmas caroling."

Books by Ida Bohatta

Bow Wow
Doctor Allsgood
Heinzel the Innkeeper
The Merry Hoppers
Shooting Stars
The Misjudged Mushroom
Barli the Ice Bear
A Day with Heinzel
The Cloud Kitchen
Velvet Paws
The Brown Family
All of the Birds

Wulli and Susi
Wixi the Easter Rabbit
The Helpful Dwarfs
Raindrops
Flipp and Flirr
The Hardworking Bee
Little Men Underground
The Busy Savers
Ice Men
The Little Advent Book
Winter House
Saint Nicholas

© 1981 ars edition, New York. All rights reserved.
Printed in West-Germany. ISBN 0-86724-024-5